pizza

pizza

SILVANA FRANCO

with photography by **WILLIAM LINGWOOD**

RYLAND
PETERS
& SMALL

LONDON NEW YORK

Author's acknowledgments

Big thanks to my trusty side-kick Annalisa Aldridge for her enthusiastic recipe testing and dough-kneading.
Also to my best friends and colleagues at Fork, Angela and Jenny, who put up with me day in, day out—
thanks girls! To my mum who fed me my first ever slice of pizza. To the very talented and patient William
Lingwood for the beautiful shots, to Vanessa Davies for the portrait and to all the team at Ryland Peters &
Small. And finally, to my brand new husband Robert—just remember, you're a very lucky man.

First published in the United States
in 2001 by Ryland Peters & Small, Inc.
519 Broadway, 5th Floor
New York, NY 10012
www.rylandpeters.com

10 9 8 7 6

Text, design, and photographs
© Ryland Peters & Small 2001

Printed and bound in China

Library of Congress
Cataloging-in-Publication Data

Franco, Silvana.
   Pizza / Silvana Franco ; with
photography by William Lingwood.
      p. cm.
   ISBN 1-84172-210-3
   1. Pizza. I. Title.

TX770.P58 F73 2001
641.8'24--dc21

          2001031859

Senior Designer
Paul Tilby

Commissioning Editor
Elsa Petersen-Schepelern

Editor
Sally Somers

Production
Patricia Harrington

Art Director
Gabriella Le Grazie

Publishing Director
Alison Starling

Food Stylist
Silvana Franco

Stylist
Liz Belton

Photographer's Assistant
Anna Bentham

NOTES

All spoon measurements are level
unless otherwise specified.
Fresh herbs are used in this book
unless otherwise stated.
If using dried herbs, halve the
quantity given.
Uncooked or partially cooked eggs
should not be served to the very old
or frail, the very young, to pregnant
women, or those with compromised
immune systems.
Ovens should be preheated to
the specified temperature. Recipes
in this book were tested with a
convexion oven.
If using a regular oven, increase the
cooking times according to the
manufacturer's instructions.

Most of the recipes in this book call
for a **pizza stone**, which is a thick,
unglazed ceramic slab. Preheated in
the oven before the pizza is added, it
is the most reliable way of producing
a perfect crisp but chewy crust.
Pizza stones are available in various
sizes from all good kitchen stores.
Alternatively, use a preheated
baking sheet.

contents

introduction

I grew up in an Italian household, where pizza always played a key role at the family table. Every month, my mother would spend a whole day pounding dough and turning out oven-sized trays of classic Margherita and calzones. For about a week, we would all snack on them at pretty well any time of day. While few of us have time to spend such long hours in the kitchen, my simple recipes for delicious homemade pizzas—enough just for two or four people—show you how easy and speedy it can be.

Once you have made a few pizzas, you'll find that you really get a feel for the texture of the dough, and will make the decision yourself as to the thickness and size of your bases. Soon, you'll find yourself being increasingly daring and inventive with your choice of toppings. Have fun, that's what cooking and eating pizza is all about!

I have only two really essential tips to share with you. Firstly, don't skimp when it comes to kneading the dough. It has to have at least 10 minutes of good, vigorous pounding to bring out its elasticity. If you don't have the energy, or you want to make a big amount, invest in a large standing electric mixer with a dough hook. Secondly, never put pizza into a cold oven—it will come out dense and soggy rather than light and crisp.

Oh—and make sure you have plenty of good red wine or ice-cold beer on hand!

basic pizza dough

Italian pizza makers use a special flour called tipo 00, available from specialty baking suppliers. If you can't find it, unbleached all-purpose flour or bread flour also make a good base. Some cooks add flavorings such as chopped herbs or grated cheese to the dough, but I like to keep it simple and let the toppings take center stage.

1²/₃ cups unbleached all-purpose flour or bread flour, plus extra for sprinkling

½ teaspoon salt

1 package active dry yeast (¼ oz.)

2 tablespoons olive oil

½ cup tepid water

SERVES 4

Put the flour, salt, and yeast in a large bowl and mix. Make a well in the center. Add the oil and water to the well and gradually work in the flour to make a soft dough. Sprinkle with a little flour if the mixture feels too sticky, but make sure it is not too dry: the dough should be pliable and smooth.

Transfer the dough onto a lightly floured surface. Knead for 10 minutes, sprinkling with flour when needed, until the dough is smooth and elastic.

Rub some oil over the surface of the dough and return the dough to the bowl. Cover with a clean cloth and leave for about 1 hour, until the dough has doubled in size.

Remove the dough to a lightly floured surface and knead for 2 minutes, until the excess air is knocked out. Roll out the dough according to the recipe you are following.

POLENTA CORNMEAL DOUGH

To make a cornmeal base, use ¹/₃ cup fine cornmeal or polenta and 1¹/₃ cups all-purpose or bread flour.

NOTE: If you are in a real hurry, use good quality frozen or fresh store-bought dough, and remember to roll it out to very thin.

basics

classic tomato sauce

This simple sauce is perfect as a basic topping for almost any pizza. Choose cans of whole plum tomatoes rather than chopped tomatoes, which can have a bitter edge. Remember to cook the sauce for at least thirty minutes to give it time to develop some richness.

Heat the oil in a small saucepan, add the shallot and garlic, and cook for about 3–4 minutes until softened. Add the tomatoes, breaking them up briefly with a wooden spoon. Add the herbs, sugar, and salt and pepper to taste.

Bring to the boil and partially cover with the lid. Reduce the heat and simmer very gently for 30–60 minutes, stirring from time to time and breaking the tomatoes down with the back of the spoon, until the sauce turns a dark red and is reduced by almost half.

Discard any woody herb sprigs. Taste and adjust the seasoning, then let cool slightly before using.

2 tablespoons olive oil

1 small onion, finely chopped

3 garlic cloves, finely chopped

28 oz. (3½ cups) canned whole plum tomatoes

2 sprigs of fresh rosemary or thyme, or a pinch of dried oregano

a pinch of sugar

salt and freshly ground black pepper

MAKES ABOUT 2 CUPS, ENOUGH FOR 8 PIZZAS

fiery tomato sauce

Hot pepper flakes add an extra kick to this smooth, satiny sauce. Use it as an alternative to the classic tomato sauce in any of these pizza recipes. The basil is not essential, but is worth adding if you have some to hand.

29 oz. (3½ cups) canned tomato sauce or purée

2 tablespoons olive oil

3 garlic cloves, finely chopped

a handful of basil leaves, torn

¼ teaspoon hot pepper flakes

½ teaspoon sugar

salt and freshly ground black pepper

MAKES ABOUT 2 CUPS,
ENOUGH FOR 8 PIZZAS

Put the tomatoes, oil, garlic, basil, pepper flakes, and sugar into a saucepan and add salt and black pepper to taste.

Bring to a boil and partially cover with a lid. Reduce the heat and simmer very gently, stirring from time to time, for 30–60 minutes, until the sauce is a dark red and reduced by about half.

Taste and adjust the seasoning, cover with the lid, and let cool slightly before using.

The secret to a delicious Marinara is in the tomatoes. Choose really ripe, plump varieties. It's well worth the extra effort of peeling and seeding them—the result is a satin-smooth, fragrant, and fruity sauce. Don't be tempted to add any cheese!

marinara

Put a pizza stone or baking sheet in the oven and preheat the oven to 425°F.

Heat 2 tablespoons of the oil in a saucepan, then add the tomatoes and salt and pepper to taste. Cook for about 5 minutes, stirring occasionally, until thickened.

Roll out the dough on a lightly floured surface to 12-inch diameter and brush with a little oil. Spoon the tomato sauce over the top and sprinkle evenly with the garlic and oregano or marjoram. Sprinkle with a little more oil.

Transfer the pizza to the hot pizza stone or baking sheet and cook for 15–20 minutes, until crisp and golden.

3–4 tablespoons olive oil

2½ cups ripe tomatoes, peeled, seeded, and diced

1 recipe pizza dough (page 8)

3 garlic cloves, very thinly sliced

1 tablespoon chopped fresh oregano or marjoram

salt and freshly ground black pepper

SERVES 4

classic pizza

margherita

The red, white, and green of this pizza—named after the queen of Italy to honor her visit to Naples just over a century ago—symbolize the *tricolore* of the Italian flag. Since the topping is so simple, try to use the best ingredients you can find.

Put a pizza stone or baking sheet in the oven and preheat the oven to 400°F.

Roll out the dough on a lightly floured surface to 12-inch diameter and brush with half the oil. Spoon the tomato sauce over it, then arrange the tomatoes and mozzarella on top.

Sprinkle the pizza with the remaining oil, salt, and plenty of pepper. Carefully transfer to the hot pizza stone or baking sheet and cook for 20–25 minutes, until crisp and golden.

Sprinkle the basil leaves over the hot pizza. Cut into wedges and serve.

1 recipe pizza dough (page 8)

2 tablespoons olive oil

1 cup classic tomato sauce (page 10)

2 cups small tomatoes, quartered or sliced

6 oz. mozzarella cheese, drained and sliced

salt and freshly ground black pepper

a handful of fresh basil leaves

SERVES 4

2 red bell peppers

2 yellow bell peppers

2 garlic cloves,
finely chopped

a small bunch of flat-leaf
parsley, finely chopped

2 tablespoons olive oil

1 recipe pizza dough
(page 8)

1 cup tomato sauce
(pages 10–11)

2 tomatoes, sliced or
halved, about 2 cups

6 oz. mozzarella cheese,
drained and sliced

salt and freshly ground
black pepper

SERVES 4

Put a pizza stone or baking sheet in the oven and preheat to 425°F. Put the peppers in a small roasting pan and bake for 30 minutes, turning them occasionally, until the skin blisters and blackens.

Meanwhile, put the garlic and parsley in a bowl. Add the oil and salt and pepper to taste.

Remove the peppers from the oven, cover with a clean cloth, and set aside for about 10 minutes, until cool enough to handle but still warm. Pierce the bottom of each pepper and squeeze the juices into the parsley and oil mixture. Peel and seed the peppers. Cut the flesh into 1-inch strips and add to the mixture in the bowl. Mix briefly, cover, and set aside at room temperature until needed.

Roll out the dough on a lightly floured surface to 12-inch diameter and brush with a little oil. Spoon the tomato sauce over the dough and arrange the tomatoes and mozzarella on top. Spoon the pepper mixture over the top.

Carefully transfer to the hot pizza stone or baking sheet and cook for 20–25 minutes, until crisp and golden. Cut into wedges and serve.

roasted bell pepper pizza

Roasting bell peppers is a very good way to bring out their sweetness. Make sure they are still warm when you add the flesh to the dressing, so that they absorb the flavors of the garlic and parsley.

mushroom with basil, chiles, and garlic oil

Mushrooms are always an excellent choice for pizza toppings. For a range of flavor and texture I like to use a mixture of varieties, including cremini, shiitake, and button. The basil-chile-garlic oil isn't essential, but adds quite a boost. If you don't care to make it, store-bought garlic, chile, or basil oil would make good substitutes.

Put a pizza stone or baking sheet in the oven and preheat the oven to 425°F.

Roll out the dough on a lightly floured surface to 12-inch diameter and brush with a little oil. Spoon the tomato sauce on top and sprinkle with the mushrooms and mozzarella.

Sprinkle the pizza with a little oil, salt, and pepper. Carefully transfer to the hot pizza stone or baking sheet and cook for 20–25 minutes, until crisp and golden.

Meanwhile, put the remaining oil in a small saucepan with the garlic and chile. Heat very gently for 10 minutes, until the garlic is softened and translucent. Remove from the heat and set aside to cool slightly for 5 minutes.

Using a fork, remove and discard the garlic and chile. Stir the basil into the flavored oil and sprinkle over the hot pizza. Cut into wedges and serve.

1 recipe pizza dough (page 8)

½ cup olive oil

1 cup tomato sauce (pages 10–11)

2½ cups thickly sliced mixed mushrooms

6 oz. mozzarella cheese, drained and diced

2 plump garlic cloves, halved

1 large, mild red chile, such as serrano, seeded and quartered

8 fresh basil leaves, finely shredded

salt and freshly ground black pepper

SERVES 4

eggplant with bresaola, arugula, and parmesan

Bresaola, dried lean beef from the Alpine region of Italy, has a lovely sweetness which here complements peppery arugula and salty Parmesan. If you can't find bresaola, use a dry-cure ham, such as prosciutto or serrano.

1 eggplant, cut into ½-inch rounds

¼ cup olive oil, plus extra to serve

1 recipe pizza dough (page 8)

1 cup tomato sauce (pages 10–11)

4 oz. very thinly sliced bresaola or cured ham

1½ cups fresh arugula leaves, torn

Parmesan cheese, freshly grated or shaved

salt and freshly ground black pepper

SERVES 4

Put a pizza stone or baking sheet in the oven and preheat the oven to 400°F. Brush the eggplant slices with the oil and sprinkle salt and pepper lightly on both sides. Preheat a stove-top grill pan, add the eggplant slices and cook for 3–4 minutes on each side, until tender and browned.

Roll out the dough on a lightly floured surface to 12-inch diameter and brush with a little oil. Spoon over the tomato sauce and arrange the eggplant slices on top.

Transfer to the hot pizza stone or baking sheet and cook for 15 minutes. Remove from the oven and ripple the bresaola or ham evenly across the pizza. Return the pizza to the oven and cook for a further 5–10 minutes, until crisp and golden.

Sprinkle with the arugula and Parmesan. Top with a splash of olive oil and a good grinding of black pepper. Cut into wedges and serve.

¼ cup olive oil

1 shallot, thinly sliced

1 cup cremini
mushrooms, sliced

2 tablespoons chopped
fresh parsley

1 recipe pizza dough
(page 8)

1 cup tomato sauce
(pages 10–11)

2 oz. prosciutto,
shredded

6 black olives

4 artichoke hearts
in brine or oil, drained
and quartered

3 oz. mozzarella cheese,
drained and sliced

4 anchovy fillets in oil,
drained

salt and freshly ground
black pepper

basil leaves, to serve

SERVES 4

quattro stagioni

The pizza for people who just can't make up their minds which one they want. You get all your favorites at once with this recipe.

Put a pizza stone or baking sheet in the oven and preheat the oven to 400°F.

Heat 2 tablespoons of the oil in a skillet, add the shallot, and cook for 2 minutes. Add the mushrooms and cook for a further 2–3 minutes, until softened and golden. Stir in the parsley and add salt and pepper to taste.

Roll out the dough on a lightly floured surface to 12-inch diameter and brush with a little oil. Spoon the tomato sauce over the top.

Pile the mushrooms over one-quarter of the pizza. Arrange the ham and olives on another quarter and the artichoke hearts on the third section of pizza. Sprinkle the mozzarella over the remaining section and put the anchovies on top. Sprinkle a little more oil over the whole pizza, then add salt and plenty of black pepper.

Carefully transfer to the hot pizza stone or baking sheet and cook for about 20–25 minutes, until crisp and golden. Cut into quarters, sprinkle the basil over the artichoke portion, and serve.

A super-thick pizza with a deep crust you can really sink your teeth into. To be sure of a crisp base, I cook this in a proper pizza pan that has holes in the bottom to allow the steam to escape.

chicago deep dish pepperoni

double recipe pizza dough (page 8)

2 tablespoons olive oil

1 cup tomato sauce (pages 10–11)

1 large tomato, sliced

1 small red onion, sliced and separated into rings

6 oz. mozzarella cheese, drained and sliced

4 oz. sliced pepperoni

salt and freshly ground black pepper

SERVES 6–8

Preheat the oven to 400°F.

Roll out the dough on a lightly floured surface to 12-inch diameter and push into a pizza pan. Brush with 1 tablespoon of the oil and spoon the tomato sauce over the top.

Arrange the tomato slices over the sauce. Sprinkle the onion rings on top, add salt and plenty of black pepper, then splash with the remaining oil. Put into the preheated oven and cook for 20 minutes.

Remove from the oven and sprinkle the mozzarella and pepperoni slices over the top. Return the pizza to the oven and cook for a further 10–15 minutes, until risen and golden. Cut into wedges and serve.

There isn't much to beat warm, freshly baked focaccia. The key to the lovely, soft texture is to cover the bread with a cloth as soon as it comes out of the oven—the steam will prevent a hard crust from forming. You can vary the ingredients by adding chopped olives, tiny cubes of cheese, or chopped fresh thyme. Focaccia is best eaten within a day or two of making.

tomato focaccia

4 cups all-purpose or bread flour

1 teaspoon table salt

1 package active dry yeast (¼ oz.)

3 tablespoons olive oil

6 sun-dried tomatoes in oil, drained and chopped

1 cup tepid water

1 teaspoon sea salt

a sprig of rosemary, chopped

2 tablespoons chile oil

SERVES 6

Put the flour, table salt, and yeast in a large bowl and mix. Make a well in the center. Add 2 tablespoons of the olive oil, the sun-dried tomatoes, and water to the well, then gradually work in the flour to make a soft dough, adding 1 tablespoon extra water if necessary. Sprinkle with a little flour if the mixture feels too sticky, but make sure it's not dry. The dough should be pliable and smooth.

Transfer the dough onto a lightly floured surface and knead for 10 minutes, sprinkling with flour when needed, until the dough is smooth and elastic.

Rub some oil over the surface and return the dough to the bowl. Cover with a cloth and leave for about 1 hour, until the mixture has doubled in size.

Remove the dough to a lightly floured surface and knead for 2 minutes, until the excess air is knocked out. Roll out the dough to make an oval, about 13 inches long. Carefully transfer to a baking sheet and cover with a clean cloth. Set aside for 30 minutes until almost doubled in size. Meanwhile, preheat the oven to 400°F.

Using your fingertips, make indents about 1 inch deep into the surface of the risen dough. Sprinkle with the remaining olive oil, then the sea salt and rosemary. Bake for 20–25 minutes, until risen and golden.

Remove the focaccia from the oven, cover with a cloth, and set aside for at least 15 minutes to cool. Sprinkle with the chile oil. Serve warm or at room temperature.

vegetarian pizza

wafer potato pizza with taleggio

A light and crispy pizza with a delicate flavor. Serve for a summer lunch with a tomato and red onion salad.

1 recipe pizza dough (page 8)

2 tablespoons olive oil

12 oz. russet potatoes

6 sage leaves, finely shredded

2 garlic cloves, crushed

7 oz. Taleggio cheese, diced

sea salt and freshly ground black pepper

SERVES 4

Put a pizza stone or baking sheet in the oven and preheat the oven to 400°F.

Divide the dough into 4 and, on a lightly floured surface, roll each piece into a wafer-thin oval, about 11 inches long. Brush the dough ovals with 1 tablespoon of the oil.

Using a mandoline, food processor, or a very sharp knife, cut the potatoes into wafer-thin slices. Put the slices into a bowl, add the sage, garlic, and remaining oil, and toss to coat. Put a single layer of potato over each dough base and sprinkle with salt and plenty of black pepper.

Carefully transfer to the hot pizza stone or baking sheet and cook for 10 minutes. Remove from the oven and sprinkle with the Taleggio. Return the pizza to the oven and cook for a further 5–10 minutes, until crisp and golden. Serve hot or warm.

charred vegetable cornmeal pizza

A robust pizza packed with flavor. Eat this straight from the oven, while the cheese is still bubbling.

Put a pizza stone or baking sheet in the oven and preheat the oven to 425°F.

Put the zucchini, eggplant, tomatoes, garlic, red onion, and thyme in a roasting pan. Add salt and pepper and sprinkle with the oil. Cook for 30 minutes, stirring from time to time, until softened and a little charred.

Lower the oven temperature to 400°F. Roll out the dough on a lightly floured surface to 12-inch diameter and spoon the vegetables over the top.

Carefully transfer the dough to the hot pizza stone or baking sheet and cook for 15 minutes. Remove from the oven and top with the dolcelatte. Return the pizza to the oven and cook for a further 5–10 minutes, until crisp and golden.

Sprinkle with the basil leaves, cut into wedges, and serve hot.

1 medium zucchini, thickly sliced

1 small eggplant, cubed

4 plum tomatoes, halved

8 unpeeled garlic cloves

1 red onion, cut into wedges

a few sprigs of thyme

2 tablespoons olive oil

1 recipe polenta pizza dough (page 8)

6 oz. dolcelatte cheese, diced

salt and freshly ground black pepper

a handful of fresh basil leaves, to serve

SERVES 4

molten cheese and gremolata calzone

Herby, zingy gremolata is wonderful with the creamy, melted cheese—quite a change from your everyday pizza-parlor calzone.

2 garlic cloves, crushed

½ cup finely chopped fresh flat-leaf parsley

grated zest of 1 lemon

1 tablespoon olive oil

14 oz. Taleggio, Brie, or Camembert cheese

double recipe pizza dough (page 8)

flour, for dusting

salt and freshly ground black pepper

SERVES 6

Put a pizza stone or baking sheet in the oven and preheat the oven to 400°F.

To make the gremolata, put the garlic, parsley, lemon zest, and oil in a bowl. Add salt and pepper to taste and mix well.

Divide the dough into 6. Put on a lightly floured surface and roll each piece into an oval about 10 inches long. Cut the cheese into 6 even slices or wedges and put a slice on one half of each dough oval. Spoon the gremolata over the cheese. Dampen the edges of the dough and fold the dough over to enclose the filling. Press the edges together firmly to seal.

Transfer to the hot pizza stone or baking sheet, dust with a little flour, and bake for 20–25 minutes, until crisp and golden. Serve hot.

fiorentina

Spinach and egg pizzas are a favorite in pizza restaurants everywhere, and you can easily make them at home. It doesn't matter if the yolk is a bit hard, but make sure it goes onto the pizza whole.

3 cups young spinach leaves

1 tablespoon butter

2 garlic cloves, crushed

1 recipe pizza dough (page 8)

1–2 tablespoons olive oil

1 cup tomato sauce (pages 10–11)

6 oz. mozzarella cheese, drained and thinly sliced

4 small eggs

½ cup finely grated fontina or Gruyère cheese

salt and freshly ground black pepper

SERVES 4

Put a pizza stone or baking sheet in the oven and preheat the oven to 425°F.

Wash the spinach thoroughly and put into a large saucepan. Cover with a lid and cook for 2–3 minutes, until the spinach wilts. Drain well and, when the spinach is cool enough to handle, squeeze out any excess water with your hands.

Melt the butter in a skillet and cook the garlic for 1 minute. Add the drained spinach and cook for a further 3–4 minutes. Add salt and pepper to taste.

Divide the dough into 4, put on a lightly floured surface and roll out each piece to about 7-inch diameter. Brush with a little oil and spoon the tomato sauce on top. Put the spinach on the bases, leaving a space in the middle for the egg. Put the mozzarella on top of the spinach, sprinkle with a little more oil, salt, and plenty of black pepper.

Carefully transfer to the hot pizza stone or baking sheet and cook for 10 minutes. Remove from the oven and crack an egg into the middle of each pizza. Top with the fontina or Gruyère and return to the oven for a further 5–10 minutes, until the base is crisp and golden, and the eggs have just set. Serve immediately.

anchovy butter and mozzarella

My favorite pizza—it always delights me that something this simple can be so loaded with flavor. I keep a roll of the anchovy butter in my freezer, so I can cut slices from the frozen roll to toss with new potatoes or pasta.

4 anchovy fillets in oil, drained

2 garlic cloves

2 tablespoons coarsely chopped flat-leaf parsley

1 tablespoon drained capers

5 tablespoons unsalted butter, at room temperature

1 recipe pizza dough (page 8)

6 oz. mozzarella cheese, drained and sliced

freshly ground black pepper

SERVES 4

Put a pizza stone or baking sheet in the oven and preheat the oven to 400°F.

Put the anchovies, garlic, parsley, and capers in a food processor and pulse until finely chopped. Remove the mixture to a bowl and add the butter. Mix well, adding plenty of black pepper. Cover and refrigerate.

Roll out the dough on a lightly floured surface to about 12-inch diameter and prick all over with a fork. Transfer to the hot pizza stone or baking sheet and cook for 15 minutes.

Remove from the oven and arrange the mozzarella over the pizza. Dot with teaspoons of the anchovy butter and return to the oven for a further 5–10 minutes, until the pizza is crisp and golden. Cut into wedges and serve.

seafood
pizza

1 lb. mussels in the shell

1 cup fresh basil leaves

10 fresh mint leaves

1 garlic clove

1 small red chile, such as serrano, seeded and coarsely chopped

grated zest of 1/2 lemon

1 tablespoon shelled pistachios

2 tablespoons freshly grated Parmesan cheese, plus extra to serve

1/3 cup olive oil

1 recipe pizza dough (page 8)

salt and freshly ground black pepper

SERVES 6

Put a pizza stone or baking sheet in the oven and preheat the oven to 400°F.

Wash the mussels thoroughly, removing the beards and discarding any with broken shells. Put into a large saucepan and cover with a tightly fitting lid. Cook over a high heat for 3–4 minutes, shaking the pan from time to time, until the shells open. Drain well, let cool, then remove the mussels from their shells. Discard the empty shells and any that have not opened.

To make the pesto, put the basil, mint, garlic, chile, lemon zest, pistachios, and Parmesan in a blender or food processor. Pulse until blended. Add the oil, salt, and plenty of black pepper and blend to a smooth paste.

Divide the dough into 6, put on a lightly floured surface, and roll out each piece to about 5-inch diameter. Brush each round with oil and prick all over with a fork. Transfer to the hot pizza stone or baking sheet and cook for 10–12 minutes.

Remove from the oven and divide the shelled mussels among the pizzette rounds. Sprinkle with pesto and return to the oven for a further 3–4 minutes, until crisp and golden. Sprinkle with Parmesan and serve warm.

mussel and pesto pizzette

Pizzette means "little pizzas." You can downscale these even further into bite-sized canapés, each with a single mussel on top. The pesto can be used in all sorts of other dishes—try stirring it into creamy mashed potatoes or risotto.

I love putting shrimp on a pizza and, although they don't go well with other kinds of cheese, I find they're fantastic with creamy mascarpone. I always use the fiery tomato sauce for this one.

shrimp and sun-dried tomato

1 recipe pizza dough (page 8)

2 tablespoons olive oil

1 cup fiery tomato sauce (page 11)

½ cup sun-dried tomatoes, chopped

½ cup mascarpone cheese

8 oz. cooked, shelled shrimp, about 8 medium

salt and freshly ground black pepper

6 scallions, finely shredded, to serve

SERVES 4

Put a pizza stone or baking sheet in the oven and preheat the oven to 400°F.

Roll out the dough on a lightly floured surface to 12-inch diameter and brush with 1 tablespoon of the oil. Spoon the tomato sauce on top and add the chopped tomatoes.

Sprinkle the pizza with the remaining oil, salt, and plenty of black pepper. Carefully transfer to the hot pizza stone or baking sheet and cook for 15 minutes.

Remove from the oven and spoon small dollops of mascarpone over the pizza. Top with the shrimp and return to the oven for a further 5–10 minutes, until crisp and golden. Sprinkle with the scallions, cut into wedges, and serve.

pizza with meat

prosciutto and fontina pizza sandwich

Sliced into long fingers or triangles and served with a simple salad, this pizza makes an elegant appetizer. Alternatively, cut into smaller pieces to serve warm with cocktails.

1 recipe pizza dough (page 8)

4 oz. prosciutto

2 cups finely grated fontina cheese

½ cup fresh arugula, torn

2 tablespoons olive oil

freshly ground black pepper

SERVES 4

Put a pizza stone or baking sheet in the oven and preheat the oven to 400°F.

Divide the dough in half, put on a lightly floured surface, and roll each half to a 10-inch square.

Layer the prosciutto on one of the squares, leaving a ½-inch border all round. Sprinkle the fontina evenly over the top, then add the arugula and black pepper.

Dampen the border with a little water and put the second square of dough on top. Press the edges firmly together to seal.

Sprinkle with oil and transfer to the hot pizza stone or baking sheet. Cook for 20–25 minutes, until crisp and golden. Cut into squares, triangles, or fingers and serve warm.

english breakfast pizza

All the best bits of a good English breakfast are right here on a pizza. The portions are hearty, so make sure you have developed a really good appetite before you start.

Put 2 pizza stones or baking sheets in the oven and preheat the oven to 400°F. Divide the dough in half, put on a lightly floured surface, and roll out each half to 8-inch diameter. Spread the mustard and ketchup over each base. Arrange the tomatoes, sausages, mushrooms, and bacon on each pizza, leaving a space in the middle for the egg.

Sprinkle with a little oil and carefully transfer to the hot pizza stones or baking sheets. Cook for 15 minutes, then remove from the oven and increase the temperature to 425°F.

Crack an egg into the middle of each pizza and sprinkle with salt and pepper. Return the pizzas to the oven and cook for a further 5–10 minutes, until the egg is just set and the base is crisp and golden. Sprinkle with the parsley and serve warm.

1 recipe pizza dough
(page 8)

2 teaspoons whole-grain
mustard

2 teaspoons tomato
ketchup

5 small tomatoes, halved
crosswise

6 pork chipolata or
breakfast sausages

5 cremini mushrooms,
halved

6 slices bacon

2 eggs

1 tablespoon olive oil

salt and freshly ground
black pepper

1 tablespoon chopped
fresh parsley, to serve

SERVES 2

topsy turvy cherry tomato pizza

Cooking a pizza upside down is a great way to make sure you get a crisp crust. It also keeps all the lovely tomato juices from escaping—the result is spectacular.

2–3 tablespoons olive oil

4 oz. pancetta or salt pork, cut into cubes

5 cups cherry tomatoes

1 recipe pizza dough (page 8)

juice of 1 lime

2 teaspoons chopped fresh mint

salt and freshly ground black pepper

jelly roll pan or baking sheet with sides, about 14 x 10 inches

SERVES 4

Preheat the oven to 400°F.

Heat 1 tablespoon of the oil in a large skillet and cook the pancetta or pork for 2–3 minutes, until golden.

Transfer the pancetta or pork and the pan oil to the jelly roll pan or baking sheet and spread around evenly. Put the cherry tomatoes in the pan, making sure that they fit in a single layer. Sprinkle with salt and pepper.

Roll out the dough on a lightly floured surface to about the same size as the pan. Put the dough on top of the tomatoes, tucking any overlap inside the pan. Bake for 20–25 minutes, until the crust is crisp and dark golden.

Meanwhile, mix the lime juice, mint, and remaining oil in a bowl.

Carefully invert the pizza onto a chopping board. Sprinkle the lime and mint mixture over the top. Slice and serve warm.

potato dough pizza
with salami and fontina

This is a lovely, chunky pizza bread. Try wrapping wedges in foil for picnics or packed lunches. If there's any left after a day or two, eat it toasted and buttered for breakfast.

Boil the potatoes in a large saucepan of salted water for 12–15 minutes, until tender. Drain well and mash thoroughly. Stir in the Parmesan, salami, yeast, salt, 2 tablespoons of the oil, flour, and enough water to make a soft dough.

Put the dough on a lightly floured surface and knead vigorously for 5 minutes, adding flour when necessary to make a smooth dough. Transfer to a baking sheet and roll out to 12-inch diameter. Cover with a clean cloth and leave for 1½ hours, until doubled in size.

Preheat the oven to 400°F. Push the diced fontina into the risen dough at regular intervals and sprinkle with the remaining oil. Bake for about 30–35 minutes, until it is cooked through and golden. Let cool for 5 minutes, then slice and serve.

10 oz. baking potatoes, such as russets, cubed

1 cup freshly grated Parmesan cheese

3 oz. sliced Italian salami, cut into fine shreds

1 package active dry yeast (¼ oz.)

1 teaspoon table salt

3 tablespoons olive oil

6 cups all-purpose or bread flour

1¼–1¾ cups tepid water

6 oz. fontina cheese, diced

salt and freshly ground black pepper

SERVES 6–8

A pizza with a distinctly Spanish flavor. As it cooks, the chorizo releases its delicious paprika juices across the pizza. I recommend using the fiery tomato sauce here. Serve with cold Spanish-style or Mexican beer.

the matador

Put a pizza stone or baking sheet in the oven and preheat the oven to 400°F.

Roll out the dough on a lightly floured surface to 12-inch diameter and brush with 1 tablespoon of the oil. Spread with the tomato sauce and arrange the pepper, chorizo, Manchego, and olives over the top.

Sprinkle the pizza with the remaining oil, salt, and plenty of black pepper. Carefully transfer to the hot pizza stone or baking sheet and cook for 20–25 minutes, until crisp and golden. Cut into wedges and serve hot.

1 recipe pizza dough (page 8)

2 tablespoons olive oil

1 cup fiery tomato sauce (page 11)

1 red bell pepper, seeded and sliced

8 oz. chorizo sausage, cut into slices about ¾ inch thick

6 oz. Manchego cheese, thinly sliced

12 black Spanish olives

salt and freshly ground black pepper

SERVES 4

The combination of rosemary, pancetta, and soft goat cheese makes a fragrant, summer pizza. This is just as good served cold, making it ideal picnic food. Serve with leafy salad greens.

pancetta, rosemary, and goat cheese pizza

1 recipe pizza dough (page 8)

2 tablespoons olive oil

8 oz. soft goat cheese

2 teaspoons coarsely chopped fresh rosemary

4 oz. cubed pancetta

salt and freshly ground black pepper

SERVES 4

Put a pizza stone or baking sheet in the oven and preheat the oven to 400°F.

Roll out the dough on a lightly floured surface to 12-inch diameter and brush with 1 tablespoon of the oil. Crumble over the cheese and top with the rosemary and pancetta.

Drizzle the pizza with the remaining oil and sprinkle with salt and plenty of black pepper. Carefully transfer to the hot pizza stone or baking sheet and cook for 20–25 minutes, until crisp and golden. Cut into wedges and serve warm, at room temperature, or cold.

1–2 tablespoons olive oil

1 lb. spicy Italian sausages

1 recipe pizza dough (page 8)

1 cup tomato sauce (pages 10–11)

1 tablespoon raisins

1 tablespoon pine nuts

6 oz. mozzarella cheese, drained and sliced

salt and freshly ground black pepper

1 scallion, thinly sliced, to serve

SERVES 4

Sicilians are famous for their use of raisins and pine nuts, one of the many legacies of Arab occupation in medieval times.

the sicilian

Heat 1 tablespoon of the oil in a large skillet and cook the sausages for 10 minutes, turning them occasionally, until nicely browned and cooked right through. Remove from the heat and let cool slightly.

Put a pizza stone or baking sheet in the oven and preheat the oven to 400°F.

Roll out the dough on a lightly floured surface to a 10-inch square and brush with a little oil.

Cut the sausage into 1-inch thick slices. Spread the tomato sauce on the pizza base and top evenly with the sausages, raisins, pine nuts, and mozzarella.

Sprinkle the remaining oil over the pizza, then add salt and plenty of black pepper. Carefully transfer to the hot pizza stone or baking sheet and cook for 20–25 minutes, until crisp and golden.

Sprinkle the scallion slices over the hot pizza, cut into wedges, and serve.

la forketta

This pizza is my own invention and has become a trademark of my company, which is called "Fork"—so I just had to include it. The fennel seeds and tangy orange zest really bring it to life.

Put a pizza stone or baking sheet in the oven and preheat the oven to 400°F.

Roll out the dough on a lightly floured surface to 12-inch diameter and brush with 1 tablespoon of the oil. Spoon over the tomato sauce and arrange the tomato slices on top. Sprinkle with the fennel seeds and half the orange zest. Top with the salami and olives.

Sprinkle the pizza with the remaining oil, salt, and plenty of black pepper. Carefully transfer to the hot pizza stone or baking sheet and cook for 20 minutes.

Remove from the oven and arrange the bocconcini over the top. Return the pizza to the oven and cook for a further 3–4 minutes, until the bocconcini have softened and started to melt, but are still keeping their shape.

Sprinkle with extra fennel seeds and the remaining orange zest. Cut into wedges and serve hot.

1 recipe pizza dough (page 8)

2 tablespoons olive oil

1 cup tomato sauce (pages 10–11)

1 large tomato, thinly sliced

a pinch of dried fennel seeds, plus extra to serve

grated zest of 1 orange

3 oz. sliced Italian salami

12 black olives

7 oz. bocconcini (baby mozzarella balls)

salt and freshly ground black pepper

SERVES 4

**1 recipe pizza dough
(page 8)**

2 tablespoons olive oil

**1 cup tomato sauce
(pages 10–11)**

**4 oz. sliced serrano ham
or prosciutto**

**3 fresh black figs,
quartered lengthwise**

**6 oz. mozzarella cheese,
drained and sliced**

3 sprigs of thyme

**salt and freshly ground
black pepper**

SERVES 4

Put a pizza stone or baking sheet in the oven and preheat the oven to 400°F.

Roll out the dough on a lightly floured surface to 12-inch diameter and brush with 1 tablespoon of the oil. Spoon over the tomato sauce and arrange the ham, fig quarters, mozzarella, and thyme on top.

Sprinkle the pizza with the remaining oil, salt and plenty of black pepper. Carefully transfer to the hot pizza stone or baking sheet and cook for 20–25 minutes until crisp and golden. Cut into wedges and serve warm.

Salty ham and sweet figs are fabulous together. Add tomatoes and you have a dramatic blaze of color.

serrano and fresh fig pizza

sweet pizza

3 peaches, halved and pitted

4 tablespoons butter, plus extra for buttering the dish

2 tablespoons dark rum

2 teaspoons brown sugar

1 recipe pizza dough (page 8)

3 oz. milk chocolate, broken into pieces

½ cup heavy cream

SERVES 6

Put a pizza stone or baking sheet in the oven and preheat the oven to 400°F.

Butter a small ovenproof dish and sit the peaches, cut-side up, in the dish. Dot with about half of the butter. Drizzle with the rum, sprinkle with the sugar, and bake for 20 minutes.

Remove from the oven and increase the oven temperature to 425°F.

Divide the dough into 6 portions, put them on a lightly floured surface, and roll out each piece to 4-inch diameter. Transfer the disks to the hot pizza stone or baking sheet. Put a peach half on each disk and sprinkle with the juices from the dish. Bake for 15 minutes until the base is golden and the peaches are soft.

Meanwhile, put the chocolate, cream, and remaining butter in a small saucepan. Heat gently, stirring all the time, until smooth.

Transfer the pizzette to small plates and drizzle with the chocolate sauce. Serve warm.

To make the most of peaches when they are at their juiciest, cook these little pizzas in summer.

chocolate and peach pizzette

raspberry and ginger crumble

**1 recipe pizza dough
(page 8)**

**1 tablespoon melted
butter**

1 cup fresh raspberries

1 teaspoon ground ginger

**4 tablespoons butter,
chilled and diced**

⅔ cup all-purpose flour

¼ cup brown sugar

2 tablespoons oatmeal

**vanilla ice cream,
to serve**

SERVES 6

Put a pizza stone or baking sheet and preheat to 400°F.

Roll out the dough on a lightly floured surface to 12-inch diameter and brush with the melted butter. Put the raspberries on the top and sprinkle with the ginger.

To make the crumble, rub the butter into the flour until the mixture looks like coarse breadcrumbs. Stir in the sugar and oats and sprinkle the mixture over the pizza.

Carefully transfer to the hot pizza stone or baking sheet and cook for 20–25 minutes until crisp and golden. Cut into wedges and serve hot with ice cream.

Raspberries and ginger go beautifully together. This pizza needs to be served hot from the oven, just as the raspberries have released their juices into the base.

strawberries and cream

A variation on a traditional summer theme, this pizza never fails to impress. Try serving it for afternoon tea on a sunny summer's day.

1 recipe pizza dough (page 8)

1 tablespoon melted butter

1 basket strawberries, halved, about 2½ cups

grated zest of 1 lemon

¼ cup confectioners' sugar

1 cup extra-thick heavy cream

2 tablespoons toasted slivered almonds, to serve

SERVES 6

Preheat the oven to 425°F.

Roll out the dough on a lightly floured surface to 13-inch diameter and brush with the melted butter.

Transfer the dough to a baking sheet. Gently push the strawberry halves into the surface of the dough at regular intervals. Sprinkle with the lemon zest and confectioners' sugar. Bake for 15 minutes until the base is golden.

Cut into wedges and top each wedge with a dollop of extra-thick cream. Sprinkle with slivered almonds and serve warm.

index

conversion charts

Weights and measures have been rounded up
or down slightly to make measuring easier.

VOLUME EQUIVALENTS:

American	Metric	Imperial
1 teaspoon	5 ml	
1 tablespoon	15 ml	
1/4 cup	60 ml	2 fl.oz.
1/3 cup	75 ml	2 1/2 fl.oz.
1/2 cup	125 ml	4 fl.oz.
2/3 cup	150 ml	5 fl.oz. (1/4 pint)
3/4 cup	175 ml	6 fl.oz.
1 cup	250 ml	8 fl.oz.

WEIGHT EQUIVALENTS: MEASUREMENTS:

Imperial	Metric	Inches	Cm
1 oz.	25 g	1/4 inch	5 mm
2 oz.	50 g	1/2 inch	1 cm
3 oz.	75 g	3/4 inch	1.5 cm
4 oz.	125 g	1 inch	2.5 cm
5 oz.	150 g	2 inches	5 cm
6 oz.	175 g	3 inches	7 cm
7 oz.	200 g	4 inches	10 cm
8 oz. (1/2 lb.)	250 g	5 inches	12 cm
9 oz.	275 g	6 inches	15 cm
10 oz.	300 g	7 inches	18 cm
11 oz.	325 g	8 inches	20 cm
12 oz.	375 g	9 inches	23 cm
13 oz.	400 g	10 inches	25 cm
14 oz.	425 g	11 inches	28 cm
15 oz.	475 g	12 inches	30 cm
16 oz. (1 lb.)	500 g		
2 1b.	1 kg		

OVEN TEMPERATURES:

110°C	(225°F)	Gas 1/4
120°C	(250°F)	Gas 1/2
140°C	(275°F)	Gas 1
150°C	(300°F)	Gas 2
160°C	(325°F)	Gas 3
180°C	(350°F)	Gas 4
190°C	(375°F)	Gas 5
200°C	(400°F)	Gas 6
220°C	(425°F)	Gas 7
230°C	(450°F)	Gas 8
240°C	(475°F)	Gas 9